Animal Farm

by
George Orwell

Student Packet

Written by:
Maureen Kirchhoefer, M.A.
Mary Lovejoy Dennis

Contains masters for:

	1	Pre-Reading Activities
	1	Study Guide
	2	Vocabulary Activities
	1	Vocabulary Quiz
	3	Comprehension Quizzes
	1	Character Analysis Activity
	1	Writing Activity
	1	Group Activity
	1	Review Activity
	1	Suggested Essay Topics
	1	Historical Review Activity
	1	Final Exam
PLUS		Detailed Answer Key

Note

The text used to prepare this guide was the Signet Classic softcover. The page references may differ in the hardcover or other paperback editions.

ISBN 1-56137-306-0

To order, contact your local school supply store, or—

Novel Units, Inc.
P.O. Box 791610
San Antonio, TX 78279

Pre-Reading Activities

The Political Novel

As students read and study *Animal Farm,* it will be very important for them to have an understanding of the political events which Orwell was satirizing. Without such an understanding, the novel can be read as little more than a sad children's story about animals. As *Animal Farm* concerns revolutions in general, it is wise to discuss in advance the reasons people revolt against their governments. Since the specific parallels in *Animal Farm* have to do with the Russian Revolution of 1917, it is necessary for students to have a basic understanding of the events and the most important political figures in those events. The Novel Units *Animal Farm Teacher's Guide* contains background information as well as a follow-up quiz. As an alternative, you may want to have the students work in cooperative study groups to research Orwell's life and times and the Russian Revolution.

Why Revolution?

Regarding revolutions in general, you might begin the unit by discussing the reasons for revolutions as a whole-class activity, or assign the topic as an impromptu essay to be done in class, with the resulting papers serving as a focal point for discussion. The important thing to grasp here is that revolutions occur when people are dissatisfied with the current conditions and when there is a leader to unite them against a real or imagined "enemy." The expectations of those who revolt are always that conditions will improve for them after the revolution. It was Orwell's opinion that revolutions were pointless because they only resulted in trading one tyrant for another due to the corrupting nature of power. Have the students contribute what they already know about life under Communist rule. The alterations in the Soviet Union under Gorbachev provide a good basis for discussion, as do the sad events in Beijing, China.

The Nature of Power

This is also a good opportunity to discuss and/or write about the concept of power. In your discussion, you might include a survey of the students to find out what has power over them. What could cause them to behave in uncharacteristic ways? The need to acquire social acceptance is a powerful influence on young people, as is the desire for expensive clothing, stereos, cars, and other material goods. Alcohol and drugs can also exert power. Have the students discuss the extent to which they feel these cultural aspects have power over young people. Then you can move on to a consideration of who holds political power in the school, the community, and the state and federal governments.

Animal Farm
Study Guide

Complete the questions as you read and study the novel. You will increase your understanding, and have a valuable tool for test review.

Chapters 1-2

1. What human characteristics (other than speech) has Orwell given to:

   Old Major

   Boxer

   Mollie

   Benjamin

   Snowball

   Napoleon

2. Why was Old Major so respected?

   What noble ideals are set forth in his dream?

   Why are the animals so excited about singing "Beasts of England"?

3. Why were the pigs immediately accepted as leaders?

   What was their motive for rebellion?

4. Who formulated the Seven Commandments? Was it done in a democratic way?

5. How well do the commandments reflect the ideas expressed in Old Major's speech?

Chapter 3

1. Did the pigs help the other animals work on the harvest?
2. Who did the animals admire the most?
3. What became his slogan?
4. Which two animals were not considered by the other animals to be good workers?
5. Which animal's character didn't seem to change at all after the Rebellion?
6. What three things happened on Sundays?
7. What did the Animal Farm flag look like? To what would it compare historically?
8. At the meetings, who never seemed to agree?
9. Who formed the animals into committees?
10. How literate were the animals? Why would literacy be an issue?
11. Who declared that the Seven Commandments could be condensed into one? What was this one maxim? Which animals would repeat this for hours?
12. Who took Jessie's and Bluebell's pups to "educate" them?
13. What had happened to the missing milk? the apples? What was Squealer's explanation?
14. What, according to Squealer, would happen if the pigs failed in their duties?
15. How do you think the disappearance of the milk and apples foreshadows future events?
16. Give some examples of the pigs' clever use of language to gain their own ends.

    a.

    b.

    c.

    d.

17. How are the animals better off after the Rebellion?

    a.

    b.

    c.

18. How are they worse off?

    a.

    b.

Chapter 4

1. How was word sent to animals on neighboring farms?
2. Name and describe the neighbors on either side of the farm.
3. How did rebelliousness show itself on other farms?
4. Early in October, Jones and men from Foxwood and Pinchfield attempted to take over Animal Farm. Who warned the animals?
5. Who has been studying Julius Caesar's campaign strategies? What was he in charge of?
6. Describe the Battle of the Cowshed.
7. Who said, "The only good human is a dead one"?
8. Who is discovered missing? Where was she found?
9. What military decorations were created? Who received them?
10. What are the anniversary dates of the Rebellion and the Battle of the Cowshed?

Chapter 5

1. What did Mollie do wrong? Where did she finally go?
2. Describe the violent debates that began to take place between Snowball and Napoleon.
3. What did Napoleon train the sheep to do with "Four legs good, two legs bad"?
4. Describe the controversy over the windmill. Why would the animals be in favor of it? Who was against it and why? Who didn't take a side on it?
5. How did Napoleon ruin Snowball's plans?
6. When Napoleon and Snowball disagreed on defense tactics, with whom did the animals agree?
7. What happened just as Snowball had the animals agreeing with him?
8. Where had the nine dogs come from?
9. What happened to Sunday meetings and debates?
10. Why was Squealer sent around to explain the new setup?
11. How did the animals react?
12. What is Boxer's new slogan?
13. To what did the animals now have to show reverence?
14. Why is it important that Napoleon, Squealer, and Minimus now sit above the other animals?
15. What do the animals learn three weeks later?
16. Why does Napoleon say he pretended to be against the windmill?
17. Who helped Squealer persuade the animals that Napoleon was right?

Chapter 6

1. In August, Napoleon announced that there would be work on Sundays. It would be strictly voluntary, but what would happen if the animals didn't work?
2. The animals were working like slaves on the windmill, yet they were happy. Why?
3. What was the main problem with building the windmill, and how was it solved?
4. How did Boxer lend extra help with the windmill?
5. Everything was operating smoothly until the animals discovered shortages of what?
6. What new policy did Napoleon announce regarding obtaining articles the farm needed?
7. What things might have to be sold in order to buy things for the windmill?
8. How would the dealings with humans be accomplished? What is a broker?
9. Describe Mr. Whymper.
10. Who set the record straight that the animals never had passed a rule against dealing with humans?
11. Why are the humans now calling the farm by its new name?
12. What rumors are circulating about Napoleon and his business agreements?
13. The pigs move where? Why is this important?
14. How did Squealer manipulate the language of the Fourth Commandment?
15. Why do the pigs get up an hour later now?
16. What happened to the windmill when it was half built?
17. What do you believe happened to the windmill? Who is being blamed?

Chapter 7

1. Why is the windmill rebuilt with walls three feet thick?
2. Who never loses heart in spite of worsening conditions?
3. Food falls short in January and starvation seems near, but it is important to <u>whom</u> not to let the outside world know?
4. What tricks are used to fool Mr. Whymper?
5. Give some examples of how Napoleon is becoming a dictator?
6. The chickens must surrender their eggs now. While their rebellion takes place, nine hens die. What are the other animals told about the nine hens?
7. Where is Snowball said to be living now?
8. What tactics does Napoleon use when negotiating the sale of the pile of lumber?
9. What animals disagreed with the explanation that Snowball was Jones' secret agent from the very beginning?
10. What explanation does Boxer accept?
11. Describe the confessions and executions.
12. What is Boxer's answer to the slaughter of other animals?
13. Give an example of Clover's blind acceptance.
14. What explanation is given for banning "Beasts of England"? What replaced it?
15. What always drowned out any animals who protested?

Chapter 8

1. What is the significance of the poem about Napoleon?
2. How has the Sixth Commandment been changed?
3. What is important about the rumor of Mr. Frederick's cruelty to his animals?
4. What is the slogan of the pigeons now?
5. What else is Snowball being blamed for?
6. Why is it ironic that the windmill is named after Napoleon?
7. Why is a death sentence decreed upon Frederick?
8. Describe the Battle of the Windmill in order of events.
9. What is ironic about their victory celebration?
10. What is the result of the pigs' discovery of whiskey?
11. What will the retirees' pasture now be used for?
12. Why is Squealer out at midnight with a ladder and paint brush?

Chapter 9

1. How is Boxer hurt? Who helps him?
2. How far away is Boxer's supposed retirement?
3. What word does Squealer use to describe the reduced rations?
4. Do the animals still believe they are free?
5. What special rights do pigs gain in this chapter?
6. What is ironic about the pigs gaining so much weight?

7. What is a Spontaneous Demonstration? What is the purpose?
8. Why was Napoleon elected president?
9. What propaganda is spread about Snowball's wound in the Battle of the Cowshed?
10. What is significant about the reappearance of Moses?
11. What type of building is going on now?
12. Why does Napoleon make arrangements to send Boxer to a "hospital"?
13. How do the pigs explain the knacker's truck? Do the animals believe them?
14. How do the pigs continue to use Boxer's strength after his death?
15. Where did the pigs get the money for the case of whiskey?

Chapter 10

1. Who is left after all these years?
2. Has anyone retired? Do you think anyone ever will?
3. What has happened to the animals' promised rewards?
4. What do the pigs have to work on, according to Squealer?
5. What does Benjamin remember about the past?
6. What new song does Napoleon now have Squealer teach the sheep?
   Why?
7. What does the wall of commandments now say?
8. What is the similarity between Napoleon and Jones?
9. Describe the conversation at the card game.
10. What is the final irony at the end of the novel?

Name______________________________

As you read the novel, write a brief definition for each of the words. Be sure you choose the correct form of the word.

scullery (15)

mincing (17)

tyranny (20)

dissentients (21)

enmity (21)

pre-eminent (25)

expounded (26)

spinney (31)

unalterable (32)

grudging (36)

parasitical (36)

obstinate (37)

cryptic (38)

tractable (46)

irrepressible (46)

ignominious (48)

posthumously (50)

pretext (51)

publican (52)

manifestly (52)

factions (55)

eloquence (57)

sordid (57)

articulate (59)

disinterred (60)

laborious (64)

arable (65)

repose (70)

perpendicularity (71)

flagstaff (71)

malignity (72)

chaff (75)

mangels (75)

infanticide (75)

capitulated (77)

coccidiosis (77)

stupefied (79)

categorically (81)

countenance (82)

retinue (89)

impending (92)

beatifically (95)

conciliatory (96)

vengeance (98)

superannuated (105)

complicity (109)

knacker (113)

morose (117)

taciturn (117)

filial (118)

imperishable (120)

deputation (123)

eminent (124)

Name______________________________

The words below are used in *reference* to the story. Write a short definition for each one.

1. fable
2. satire
3. irony
4. totalitarianism
5. capitalism
6. proletariat
7. bourgeoisie
8. idealist
9. scapegoat
10. broker

Name______________________________

Match the letter of the correct definition with the word it defines.

______ 1. fable

_____ 2. satire

_____ 3. irony

_____ 4. totalitarianism

_____ 5. capitalism

_____ 6. proletariat

_____ 7. bourgeoisie

_____ 8. idealist

_____ 9. scapegoat

_____ 10. broker

a. person paid a fee for acting as an agent in making sales
b. one who bears the blame for others
c. one party/group controlling a government
d. one who sees things as they could be rather than as they are
e. an economic system where individuals own businesses
f. the property-owning class
g. a short tale designed to teach a moral
h. a figure of speech in which the literal meaning is the opposite of the intended meaning
i. literary device using wit, derision or irony to criticize weakness or wrong-doing
j. a group which has nothing to sell but its labor; the working class

Name______________________________

Match the following fictional creations with the real things they represent.

_____	1. Foxwood	a.	Czar Nicholas II
_____	2. Major	b.	Hitler's Germany
_____	3. Jones	c.	Russian Orthodox Church
_____	4. Napoleon	d.	Marx-Lenin
_____	5. Snowball	e.	Stalin
_____	6. Moses	f.	Trotsky
_____	7. Squealer	g.	propaganda ministry
_____	8. Boxer & Clover	h.	secret police
_____	9. fierce dogs	i.	workers (proletariat)
_____	10. Pinchfield	j.	U.S.S.R.
_____	11. Manor Farm	k.	Imperial Russia (1917)
_____	12. Animal Farm	l.	Britain

True-False: Decide whether the statements are true or false. Remember that to be true a statement must be completely true. Write out the words "true" and "false."

_____ 13. Major's dream of the future as given in his speech is a deliberate plot to enslave the animals.

_____ 14. Jones suspects that the animals are plotting a revolt

_____ 15. "Animalism" is the code that ranked the farm animals into social classes.

_____ 16. Animalism was the creation of a representative group of animals.

_____ 17. The cat takes a firm stand on all resolutions brought up at the meetings.

_____ 18. The animals were inspired by Old Major's speech.

_____ 19. Napoleon and Snowball cooperate to get Animal Farm running smoothly.

Name_______________________________

_____ 20. The disappearance of the milk immediately after the Rebellion is due to the greediness of the now-untrained sheep.

_____ 21. The main battle of the Rebellion took the animals by surprise.

_____ 22. Old Major formulated the Seven Commandments of Animalism as "unalterable law."

_____ 23 Orwell's central problem in human relations was how to prevent power from becoming abused.

_____ 24. Moses is an enemy of the Rebellion.

_____ 25. After the Rebellion, the animals spend much time celebrating and are reluctant to work on "their" farm.

_____ 26. At first the animals shamelessly stole food.

_____ 27. The single maxim of "Animalism" is "Two legs good, four legs bad."

_____ 28. Boxer is a valued member of the community because of his great intelligence.

Multiple Choice: Circle the letter of each correct choice.

29. The leader who was an idealist with the good of all the animals as his aim was
    a. Snowball b. Squealer c. Napoleon d. Major
30. Mollie's lack of cooperation in the Rebellion was due to her
    a. love for Boxer b. love for ribbons and sugar c. dislike for pigs
31. All of the following are principles of Animalism except "No animal shall...
    a. wear clothes b. drink alcohol c. be corrupted by power d. sleep in a bed
32. Squealer's explanation for the pigs' need for milk and apples is
    a. they need rewards for their work
    b. they don't really like them but need them to keep their brain power
    c. they need them to trade for materials for the windmill
    d. they will store them for all the animals to eat in winter
33. After the Rebellion the animals decided to make the farmhouse into a
    a. recreation area b. school for the young c. headquarters d. museum
34. When an animal outlived its usefulness under Jones it usually was
    a. killed b. put out to pasture c. sold d. made into dog food
35. Jones' bad traits include all of the following except
    a. drinking b. carelessness c. cruelty d. jealousy

Name______________________________

Choose the best answer to each of the following.

1. The way in which the animals spread the news of the rebellion to the neighboring farms and tried to subvert the other animals was through the
   a. dogs b. pigeons c. pigs d. sheep
2. After the Rebellion, Mr. Jones spent his time
   a. planning a vicious counter-attack b. drinking and complaining at the tavern
   c. moving out of town d. working hard to build a new farm
3. Mr. Pilkington of Foxwood, an "easy going gentleman farmer," symbolizes
   a. Orwell b. Churchill c. Hitler d. Marx
4. Mr. Frederick of Pinchfield, a "tough, shrewd man, perpetually involved in lawsuits," symbolizes
   a. Hitler b. Nicholas c. Churchill d. Orwell
5. The animals learn of Jones' attempt to recapture the farm from
   a. Jones b. the cat c. Pilkington d. the pigeons
6. The award, "Animal Hero, First Class," was given to
   a. Napoleon and Snowball b. Snowball and Boxer
   c. Napoleon and Boxer d. only Boxer
7. The farmhouse symbolizes
   a. evil b. nature c. safety d. knowledge
8. The animal who becomes a traitor to the farm is
   a. Boxer b. Squealer c. Benjamin d. Mollie
9. The conflict between Snowball and Napoleon erupts into a violent debate over
   a. education b. committees c. work schedules d. the windmill
10. The only animal who did not take a side on the issue of the windmill was
    a. Benjamin b. Boxer c. Moses d. Clover
11. After Snowball was driven out, Napoleon immediately cancelled the
    a. weekly debates b. flag raising ceremonies
    c. "anthem" singing d. weekly day of rest
12. The one who explains to the animals the reasons for the changes is
    a. Napoleon b. Boxer c. Moses d. Squealer
13. The animals were surprised when Napoleon
    a. argued with Snowball b. took over Snowball's windmill plans
    c. drove Snowball crazy d. was killed
14. After Napoleon takes over, the animals are required to pay special reverence to
    a. Major's skull b. Jones' whip c. Napoleon's trotter d. the dogs
15. As his logical successor, Old Major would probably have favored ____________ as being most consistent with his own ideas and policies.
    a. Napoleon b. Snowball c. Squealer d. Mollie

Name______________________________

Matching: Write the letter of the correct character next to his/her description.

a.	Whymper
b.	Muriel
c.	neighboring animals
d.	Boxer
e.	Mollie
f.	Napoleon
g.	Snowball
h.	Frederick
i.	Benjamin
j.	the nine dogs

_____ 16. One of the next-door neighbors.

_____ 17. Lured away from the farm by a human.

_____ 18. A broker hired to arrange trade with humans.

_____ 19. Originator of the windmill plan.

_____ 20. "I will work harder."

_____ 21. A goat who can read quite well.

_____ 22. Cynical and non-committal.

_____ 23. Showed signs of rebellion.

_____ 24. Pronounces death sentence on Snowball.

_____ 25. Enforcers of Napoleon's rules.

True-False: Write "true" next to true statements and "false" next to statements which are false. Remember to read each statement carefully.

________ 26. Neighboring farmers were not bothered by the Rebellion at Animal Farm.

________ 27. Snowball had studied an old book of Julius Caesar's war campaigns.

________ 28. Boxer was disappointed he hadn't killed the stable boy.

________ 29. Snowball had a flair for making brilliant speeches.

________ 30. The purpose of the windmill was to mechanize the farm.

Short Answer: Answer each question briefly.

31. How were the animals able to break the pieces of stone into manageable pieces?

32. How did the pigs change the Fourth Commandment, *"No animal shall sleep in a bed"?*

33. What "evidence" was offered to support Napoleon's opinion of who had destroyed the windmill?

Name_______________________________

Choose the best answer for each question.

1. Rebuilding the windmill was harder because
   a. of the snow   b. the walls had to be thicker
   c. the animals were cold and hungry   d. all of these
2. Through Whymper, Napoleon had accepted a contract for
   a. 10 bushels of potatoes per week   b. 400 eggs per week
   c. 60 gallons of milk per month   d. all of these
3. When anything went wrong, it was usually attributed to
   a. Minimus   b. Squealer   c. Major   d. Snowball
4. The animal who found it hardest to believe Snowball had been a traitor at the Battle of the Cowshed was
   a. Muriel   b. Boxer   c. Clover   d. Benjamin
5. Which of the animals confessed to crimes first?
   a. a sheep   b. three hens   c. a goose   d. four pigs
6. The Sixth Commandment was changed by adding
   a. "at the farm"   b. "in cold blood"   c. "without cause"   d. "in front of others"
7. Napoleon decreed that the gun be fired on
   a. Squealer's birthday   b. Lenin's birthday   c. Boxer's birthday   d. his birthday
8. Every stroke of good fortune on the farm was
   a. because of Boxer   b. celebrated   c. attributed to Napoleon   d. all of these
9. Pilkington's reply to Napoleon's conciliatory message was
   a. "I forgive you."   b. "Live and let live."   c. "Serves you right."   d. none of these
10. The men who destroyed the second windmill had
    a. guns   b. dynamite   c. a crowbar   d. all of these
11. After the destruction of the second windmill, Boxer began looking forward to
    a. rebuilding the third   b. a heated stall   c. retirement   d. visiting the knacker
12. Squealer fell when he was
    a. changing a commandment   b. planting barley
    c. running through the barnyard   d. walking on two legs
13. The vote for Napoleon for President was
    a. 10-4   b. 8-6   c. unanimous   d. 9-5
14. In what ways did the animals lives <u>not</u> change?
    a. slept on straw   b. labored   c. were cold and hungry   d. all of these
15. The quarrel at the end of the novel resulted from
    a. cheating at cards   b. counterfeit money   c. excessive drinking   d. all of these

Name______________________________

Short Answer: Write a brief answer for each question.

16. Explain one of the tricks used to convince Whymper and the outside world that conditions at the farm were good.

17. How was the Fifth Commandment ("No animal shall drink alcohol.") changed, and why?

18. What information was circulated about Snowball?

19. What explanation were the animals given about Boxer being taken away from the farm? Why did they choose to believe it?

20. When the animals were told that Napoleon was dying, what was the real problem?

True-False: Write "true" if the statement is true. Write "false" if it is false.

________ 21. Nine hens died of coccidiosis.

________ 22. Whymper told Napoleon over and over not to sell the timber.

________ 23. Snowball was reported to be Jones' secret agent.

________ 24. Boxer was surprised when three dogs attacked him.

________ 25. An extra verse was added to "Beasts of England."

________ 26. The bank notes received for the timber were worth $10,000.

________ 27. The leisure the animals dreamed of never came to pass.

________ 28. After the timber deal, Napoleon and Frederick became trusted friends.

________ 29. The sheep were great devotees of Spontaneous Demonstrations.

________ 30. Benjamin was very upset when the knacker came for Boxer.

________ 31. At the end of the novel, the animals could still tell the men from the pigs.

Character Interactions

Just like people in real life, characters in novels act differently around some characters than they do around others. Fill in the Character Interaction Chart, below, for Boxer. Then choose another character and make your own chart.

Along the lines going TO Boxer, write how that character feels and acts toward him. On the lines going AWAY from Boxer, write how Boxer feels and acts toward the character.

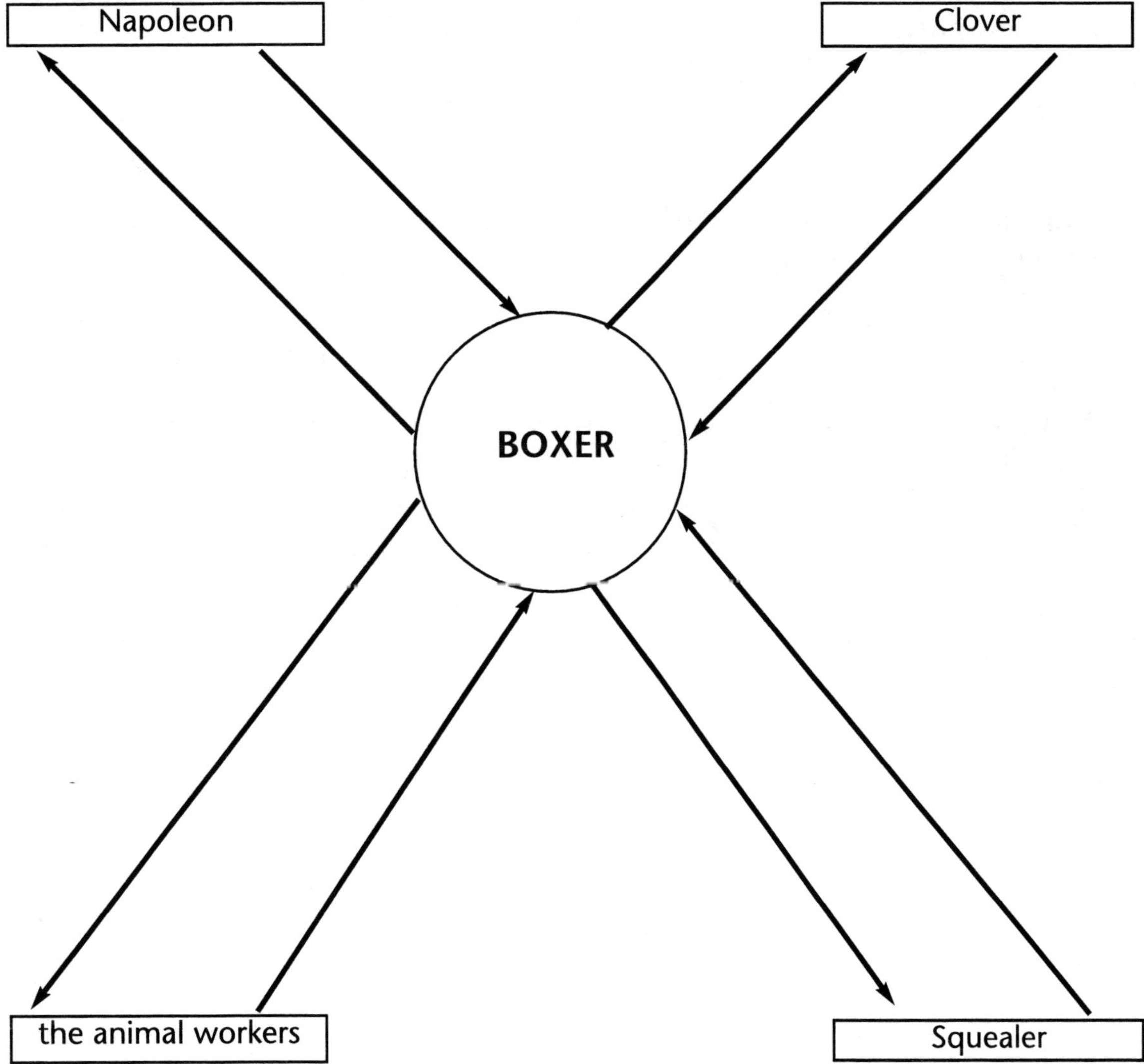

Write Your Own Fable

Orwell used animal characters to represent real people, and events in *Animal Farm* to stand for real events to which he was opposed. You have probably watched shows on television which satirize current events and people in much the same way. Now is your chance to make your own subtle statements about a situation or event you would like to satirize. This worksheet will help you to organize your thoughts, plan your characters, and outline your plot.

1. First, think of a situation or event you would like to satirize:

   ____

2. Think carefully about the people you will include in your fable. Then decide what animals you will use to represent them.

Characters

Real People	Represented by What Animals?

3. Orwell used Manor Farm/Animal Farm as his setting. Describe the setting you will use.

   ____

   ____

4. On the back of this page, make a brief plot outline. Be sure to include the following: Exposition, Rising Action, Climax, Falling Action, Dénouement (or ending).

5. You're now ready to write your fable.

Each group is to analyze ONE of the last five chapters of Animal Farm. EACH member of the group is responsible for one part of the analysis. This analysis should include the answers to such questions as:

1. What action of the plot occurs in this chapter?

2. What do these incidents of the plot illustrate about the relations of an individual to the state?

3. What do these incidents of the plot illustrate relative to the Seven Commandments and Major's speech in the first two chapters?

4. What has happened as far as the difference between the pigs and the other animals is concerned?

5. Irony is achieved by saying or writing the opposite of what is really meant. What irony is found in this chapter?

6. What significant details do you find in this chapter? Why are they significant?

7. What are the parallels to Russian history found in this chapter?

REMEMBER:

- This presentation is to be done in a panel in front of the rest of the class.
- Speak clearly so that the class can understand you.
- Put some time into your preparation—you'll have more confidence.

You will receive a group grade, so make sure that each group member is contributing his or her best effort.

Circle your group assignment below and write in the date due.

GROUP #1 Chapter 6 Due ______________
GROUP #2 Chapter 7 Due ______________
GROUP #3 Chapter 8 Due ______________
GROUP #4 Chapter 9 Due ______________
GROUP #5 Chapter 10 Due ______________

Name________________________________

Create a title for each chapter. Then write the most important events of the chapter under the title.

Chapter 1 Title: ________________________________

Important events: ________________________________

____

Chapter 2 Title: ________________________________

Important events: ________________________________

____

Chapter 3 Title: ________________________________

Important events: ________________________________

____

Chapter 4 Title: ________________________________

Important events: ________________________________

____

Chapter 5 Title: ________________________________

Important events: ________________________________

____

Chapter 6 Title: ________________________________

Important events: ________________________________

____

Chapter 7 Title: ________________________________

Important events: ________________________________

____

Chapter 8 Title: ________________________________

Important events: ________________________________

____

Chapter 9 Title: ________________________________

Important events: ________________________________

____

Chapter 10 Title: ________________________________

Important events: ________________________________

____

Suggested Essay Topics

Choose one of the topics below for your paper. Be sure to cite specific examples to support your statements. Generalities are not acceptable.

1. Discuss irony as it is used in *Animal Farm.* Be sure to give specific examples from the novel.

2. Orwell felt that revolutions fail in that they result only in a change of tyrants. Use specific examples to trace Napoleon's rise to power and show how he is an excellent example of Orwell's philosophy.

3. Decide whether or not you think Squealer is free. Then explain your opinion and support it with details and examples from the book.

4. Find examples of humor in *Animal Farm.* Explain what purpose humor serves in the novel. How does it support Orwell's theme?

5. Give a brief summary of the essential plot of *Animal Farm*—the "what happens." In order to do this, you will first have to decide which are major and which are minor episodes in the story and be sure you have a clear idea of the theme.

6. Explain what happened to each of the Seven Commandments.

7. How has Orwell used the animal fable to present his view of human nature? Back up any generalizations you make with specific scenes and characters.

8. With what ideas and with which characters is Orwell most in sympathy? How does he show his sympathy?

9. Examine the use of propaganda to control the animals and their thinking.

10. Boxer exemplifies Orwell's idea that simple creatures work harder and harder for causes they cannot admit no longer exist. Show how this is true for Boxer. What cause is he fighting for, and in what ways can one say that this cause is dead?

Name______________________________

Match the historical event with the appropriate *Animal Farm* counterpart.

_______ 1. Marx-Lenin

_______ 2. Stalin

_______ 3. England

_______ 4. Czar Nicholas II

_______ 5. Trotsky

_______ 6. Russian Revolution of 1917

_______ 7. Lenin's body

_______ 8. Propaganda agent

_______ 9. Blood purges of 1936-38

_______ 10. White Russians

_______ 11. proletariat

_______ 12. Teheran conference

_______ 13. Five year plan

_______ 14. Germany

_______ 15. Foreign agent

a. Mr. Whymper
b. Squealer
c. animals other than pigs and dogs
d. animal confessions
e. Snowball
f. four young porkers
g. Mr. Jones
h. Pinchfield Farm
i. Foxwood Farm
j. Old Major
k. Napoleon
m. Old Major's skull
n. building the windmill
o. card party with men and pigs
p. Animal Rebellion

Name______________________________

Choose the best answer for each question.

1. One main point of Major's speech was that under Jones their lives are
   a. easy, but long
   b. difficult, but rewarding
   c. dignified and comfortable
   d. miserable, laborious, and short

2. Major stated that the only creature who consumes without producing is
   a. birds
   b. pigs
   c. man
   d. sheep

3. The Rebellion, although it had been talked about and planned, actually took place rather spontaneously because of
   a. Jones' weakness, vice, and neglect
   b. Old Major's death
   c. Moses' departure
   d. the farm hands' oversight in leaving the barn unlocked

4. Immediately after the Rebellion, it was learned that the pigs had
   a. stolen several guns
   b. taught themselves to read and write
   c. planned to overtake other farms
   d. learned to walk on two legs

5. The work of teaching and organizing the others fell naturally upon the pigs, who were generally recognized as being the
   a. largest group of animals
   b. strongest group of animals
   c. wildest group of animals
   d. cleverest group of animals

6. Early in October of the first year Jones and all his men attempted to
   a. steal some supplies from the farm
   b. recapture the farm
   c. tour Animal Farm for enlightenment
   d. assassinate Snowball

7. After studying an old book of Julius Caesar's campaigns, ____________ took charge of the defensive operations against Jones and his men.
   a. Napoleon
   b. Boxer
   c. Snowball
   d. Squealer

8. The animals were victorious because of
   a. a capable leader
   b. an ambush
   c. their strong spirit
   d. all of these

9. There was a rivalry for command between
   a. Boxer and Clover
   b. Snowball and Napoleon
   c. Squealer and Napoleon
   d. Mollie and Snowball

10. During discussions at their meetings, the animals usually agreed with
    a. Boxer
    b. Snowball
    c. Napoleon
    d. whomever was speaking

11. ___________ was chased off the farm by nine fierce dogs.
   a. Napoleon   b. Mollie   c. Snowball   d. Benjamin

12. The windmill was soon begun. The most difficult part of the animals' task comes in
   a. deciding whose plans to follow   b. hooking up their radios
   c. breaking up the stone   d. getting Boxer to do his share

13. Led by Frederick, several men banded together to attack Animal Farm. Their prime target is the
   a. barn   b. windmill   c. pigs' houses   d. grain bins

14. The thing that spurred the animals' courage in the last battle was
   a. Boxer's speech   b. their preparation in war tactics
   c. their hatred of Snowball   d. the sight of the spot where the windmill had been

15. In the last chapter the pigs changed the name of their farm to
   a. Manor Farm   b. Animal Estate   c. Napoleon Manor   d. Pig Palace

16. "The creatures outside looked from pig to man, and from man to pig, and from pig to man again; but already it was impossible to say which was which." This statement shows
   a. the creatures' vision is blurred   b. the men have revered Old Major's goals
   c. the supreme irony of the Rebellion   d. the creatures are stupid animals

17. Orwell makes this statement about power in *Animal Farm:*
   a. Power comes to those who refuse to abandon their ideals of equality.
   b. Power corrupts, and absolute power corrupts absolutely.
   c. Physical force is not needed to maintain power or control.
   d. Men do not respect the power of the bourgeoisie.

18. A theme regarding education in *Animal Farm* is
   a. Education is unimportant to society.
   b. A rebellion can occur only after the masses are educated.
   c. Educated rulers work for the good of the society.
   d. Democracy needs a good memory and good education to resist those who would forcefully rule.

19. Orwell implies that, had Snowball taken over the farm instead of Napoleon, the ending would have been no different. This is what kind of view of life?
   a. optimistic   b. happy   c. hopeful   d. pessimistic

20. A characteristic of man is to establish rules by which to live, and that characteristic is paralleled by
    a. Squealer's techniques of persuasion
    b. the Seven Commandments
    c. "Beasts of England"
    d. the plans for the windmill

21. Man's tendency to blindly believe an authoritarian figure despite facts to the contrary is pictured in one of the animals' beliefs that
    a. Moses was sent to turn the animals against Napoleon
    b. Snowball was a better leader than Napoleon
    c. Napoleon was always right
    d. the sheep were Napoleon's secret police

22. The animals mirror a human characteristic of being led astray by figures when Squealer
    a. presents blueprints of the windmill
    b. uses statistics to prove what he tells the animals
    c. sends out large numbers of pigeons to broadcast the Rebellion
    d. keeps accurate figures on the amount of milk and animals the pigs consume

23. Often the problem with a dictatorship, as shown by the pigs, is that
    a. the dictator becomes more and more thirsty for power
    b. the common worker becomes dissatisfied with members of the proletariat
    c. capitalism has only one class of people
    d. government of the people, by the people, and for the people has never really worked

24. Benjamin represents a human being who
    a. never pitches in to get the job done
    b. is always full of clever expressions and slogans
    c. is extremely cynical about everything
    d. lives life to the fullest

25. One of Mollie's qualities is
    a. intelligence
    b. vanity
    c. curiosity
    d. eagerness

26. Orwell's belief that revolution is ultimately doomed to failure is shown by
    a. the way the other farmers keep attacking Animal Farm
    b. the way Old Major's ideas become corrupted by the pigs' hunger for power
    c. the animals' happiness immediately after the Rebellion
    d. Napoleon's agreement, finally, to allow Boxer, Clover, and Benjamin to retire

27. Idealism is pictured in the character of
    a. Napoleon   b. Old Major   c. the hens   d. Squealer

28. Orwell believed that in a society of class distinction the lower class is always the loser. This is shown in the story by
    a. Benjamin's fate
    b. the way the dogs are trained privately by Napoleon
    c. the treatment of Boxer when he becomes ill
    d. Mr. Frederick's lack of honesty in dealing with the animals

29. Orwell's belief that Russian Communism was no better than the oppressive rule of the Czar is shown by
    a. Napoleon's brutality and the increased submission of the animals
    b. Frederick and Pilkington's refusal to establish formal relations with Animal Farm
    c. the death of Moses
    d. Squealer's continued use of sound reasoning to change the animals' minds

Irony

30. Irony is a figure of speech
    a. in which the characters take on human characteristics
    b. used for the purpose of spreading a particular doctrine
    c. which uses a mild indirect expression for a harsh or blunt one
    d. in which the literal meaning is opposite of what is intended

31. What is the irony of the following statement in reference to the problems and tragedies on the farm: "It must be due to some fault in ourselves"?
    a. Boxer does not realize the "fault" is the pigs' corruption
    b. Boxer does not put the blame where it really belongs—on Moses
    c. Boxer blames himself and the others when the blame belongs on Snowball
    d. Napoleon has really caused all the difficulties by working with Jones

32. The actions of the pigs are ironic in that
    a. the pigs aren't really the smartest animals on the farm
    b. they parallel the actions of Farmer Jones
    c. the other animals are hungry and tired
    d. the pigs work very hard physically on the windmill

Use of Language

33. When Snowball reduced the Seven Commandments to a single maxim: "Four legs good, two legs bad," he was guilty of the logical fallacy of
    a. irony b. euphemism c. over-simplification d. card-stacking

34. When Squealer tells the animals that the pigs must sleep in beds or else Jones will come back, he is using
    a. euphemism
    b. irony
    c. faulty cause-and-effect reasoning
    d. bandwagon appeal

35. The final slogan of Animalism, "All animals are equal, but some animals are more equal than others" suffers what logical fallacy?
    a. faulty cause-and-effect reasoning
    b. euphemism
    c. internal contradiction
    d. over-simplification

36. The original Seven Commandments were changed in order to
    a. correct any errors
    b. fit the pigs' purposes
    c. benefit all of the animals
    d. make them easier to understand

37. Squealer states that he actually dislikes milk and apples. Even though this is "true" he must eat them because
    a. they are the only types of food available
    b. it has been ordered by Napoleon
    c. he is a brain-worker and must preserve his health
    d. they cannot be wasted

38. Napoleon was the character who gave the orders, but Squealer was the one who
    a. cleaned the barn
    b. drank all the milk and ate all the apples
    c. had to rationalize the orders to the others
    d. first carried a cane

39. Throughout *Animal Farm,* the sheep and Boxer use slogans. This is dangerous to the planned outcome of the revolution because
    a. it hurts the other animals' feelings
    b. it keeps them working
    c. they use the slogans without thinking or understanding
    d. slogans should only be used in advertising

Fable

Mark A if the statement is a characteristic of a FABLE. Mark B if it is not a characteristic.

_____ 40. The major character rises from a humble background to a position of power.

_____ 41. The characters are animals with human characteristics.

_____ 42. Fables are tales usually told to point out a lesson.

43. The use of the fable form
    a. prevents the use of satire
    b. was suggested to Orwell at his preparatory school
    c. enabled Orwell to slightly disguise the target of his book
    d. results in the loss of any serious message

44. The use of the fable form enabled Orwell to do all of the following except
    a. point out human weaknesses by attributing them to animals
    b. present a serious message in a light-hearted manner
    c. describe a legendary hero
    d. provide a moral about the use of power

WHO said the following?

45. "You don't want Jones back, do you?"
    a. Boxer   b. Napoleon   c. Sheep   d. Squealer

46. (When Boxer is taken away) "Fools! Fools! Do you not see what is written on the side of that van?"
    a. Clover   b. Boxer   c. Benjamin   d. Moses

47. "Our Leader, Comrade Napoleon...has stated categorically—categorically, comrade,—that Snowball was Jones' agent from the very beginning."
    a. Squealer   b. Pinkeye   c. Jones   d. Snowball

48. "Four legs good, two legs bad" repeated again and again.
    a. Napoleon   b. Benjamin   c. sheep   d. dogs

Match the following.

________	49	Marx-Lenin	a. Farmer Jones
________	50.	Czar Nicholas II	b. Pinchfield (Frederick)
________	51.	Germany	c. Pilkington (Foxwood)
________	52.	Trotsky	d. Old Major
			e. Snowball

________	53.	Stalin	a. Squealer
________	54.	Teheran Conference	b. Battle of the Cowshed
________	55.	Propaganda agent	c. Napoleon
________	56.	Russian Revolution of 1917	d. Rebellion
			e. card party

57. When a government is controlled by one party or group, it is referred to as a/an _______________ government.
    a. totalitarian b. bourgeoisie c. capitalistic d. republican

58. Because Boxer felt that if he worked harder and got up earlier in the morning everything would turn out all right, he is considered a/an
    a. sadist b. realist c. idealist d. pessimist

59. Marx felt that there existed in society a group of people who had nothing to sell but their labor. He referred to this group of people as the
    a. management b. middle class c. bourgeoisie d. proletariat

60. Marx referred to the property owning class as the
    a. proletariat b. elite c. bourgeoisie d. lucky

61. All of the blame for everything that went wrong on the farm was placed on Snowball. He was Napoleon's
    a. scapegoat b. adversary c. compatriot d. peer

62. Squealer's use of "readjustment" instead of "reduction" in food rations so that the animals would not become upset is an example of
a. satire b. irony c. simile d. euphemism

63. Although Benjamin knew what was going on, he rarely spoke. He could be termed
a. enmity b. taciturn c. scapegoat d. militant

64. A piece of writing that holds up to ridicule and contempt the weaknesses and wrong-doing of individuals, groups, or humanity is called
a. a farce b. a comedy c. a satire d. irony

65. Mr. Whymper acted as a go-between for the pigs and therefore was their
a. enmity b. idealist c. cynical d. broker

Essay Questions.

As you write your answers to the essay questions, remember to cite specific examples and details from the novel.

A. Describe the situation depicted in the last scene of *Animal Farm.* How does it effectively represent Orwell's feelings about revolution?

B. Explain who Boxer represents and how his tragedy fits into Orwell's story about revolution.

C. Describe at least three instances of the pigs' disobeying the Seven Commandments of Animalism.

Answer Key

Vocabulary II Quiz

1.	G	6.	J
2.	I	7.	F
3.	H	8.	D
4.	C	9.	B
5.	E	10.	A

Chapters 1-3 Quiz

1.	L	19.	false
2.	D	20.	false
3.	A	21.	false
4.	E	22.	false
5.	F	23.	true
6.	C	24.	true
7.	G	25.	false
8.	I	26.	false
9.	H	27.	false
10.	B	28.	false
11.	K	29.	D
12.	J	30.	B
13.	false	31.	C
14.	false	32.	B
15.	false	33.	D
16.	false	34.	A
17.	false	35.	D
18.	true		

Chapters 4-6 Quiz

1.	B	19.	G
2.	B	20.	D
3.	B	21.	B
4.	A	22.	I
5.	D	23.	C
6.	B	24.	F
7.	A	25.	J
8.	D	26.	false
9.	D	27.	true
10.	A	28.	false
11.	A	29.	true
12.	D	30.	true
13.	B	31.	by dropping them off cliff
a 14.	A		
15.	B	32.	They added "with sheets."
16.	H		
17.	E	33.	The tracks of a pig led into the hedge
18.	A		

Chapters 7-10 Quiz

1.	D	17.	"To excess" was added. Pigs were now drinking.
2.	B		
3.	D		
4.	B	18.	He had been Jones' agent from beginning.
5.	B		
6.	C		
7.	D	19.	Knacker's van was really vet's; Boxer died in hospital. Easier to accept.
8.	C		
9.	C		
10.	D		
11.C		20.	Had a hangover.
12.	A		
13.	C		(see left box)
14	D		
15.	A		
16.	Animals discussed their success in his hearing; grain bins filled with sand.		

Chapters 7-10 Quiz, cont.

21.	false	27.	true
22.	false	28.	false
23.	true	29.	true
24.	true	30.	true
25.	false	31.	false
26.	false		

Historical Review

1.	J	6.	P	11.	C
2.	K	7.	M	12.	O
3.	I	8.	D	13.	N
4.	G	9.	B	14.	H
5.	E	10.	F	15.	A

Final Exam

1.	D	21.	C	41.	A	61.	A
2.	C	22.	B	42.	A	62.	D
3.	A	23.	A	43.	C	63.	B
4.	B	24.	C	44.	C	64.	C
5.	D	25.	B	45.	D	65.	D
6.	B	26.	B	46.	C		
7.	C	27.	B	47.	A		
8.	D	28.	C	48.	C		
9.	B	29.	A	49.	D		
10.	D	30.	D	50.	A		
11.	C	31.	A	51.	B		
12.	C	32.	B	52.	E		
13.	B	33.	C	53.	C		
14.	D	34.	C	54.	E		
15.	A	35.	C	55.	A		
16.	C	36.	B	56.	D		
17.	B	37.	C	57.	A		
18.	D	38.	C	58.	C		
19.	D	39.	C	59.	D		
20.	B	40.	B	60.	C		

Essays (Students' answers will vary.)

A. In the last scene of the novel, the neighboring farmers are playing cards with the pigs, and the animals are unable to tell the pigs from the humans. Orwell used this scene to show that once the pigs gained power, they were no different from the tyrannical Jones. In Orwell's view, all revolutions are doomed to fail because of the corrupting nature of power.

B. Boxer represents the proletariat. His tragedy—being used in his illness for still further financial gain after being promised retirement—exemplifies how the system of Communism uses the worker as a tool to glorify and enrich the state.

C. The pigs eventually disobeyed all of the Seven Commandments by exploiting their fellow animals, killing them, dealing with humans, sleeping in beds, wearing clothes, drinking alcohol, walking on two legs, and finally changing the seventh commandment to "All animals are equal, but some are more equal than others."

Study Guide

Chapters 1-2

1. Old Major - persuasive, fatherly
   Boxer - hard-working, trusting, not too bright
   Mollie - vain, selfish, stupid
   Benjamin - cynical, intellectual
   Snowball and Napoleon - tyrannical, power-hungry
2. Old Major was the oldest Middle White Boar. The noble ideals in his dream include the end of the exploitation of animals and the equality of all animals. "Beasts of England" gives the animals a feeling of hope about the future and unifies them.
3. The pigs were considered to be very clever. Their motive was to get the farm away from humans, but they have an additional motive—power over the other animals. Students may not be aware of this underlying motive at this point.
4. The pigs formulated the Seven Commandments. No, the others were not consulted.
5. The commandments seem to reflect the ideas expressed in Old Major's speech, but the act that the pigs are clearly gaining power is a problem.

Chapter 3

1. No. They directed and supervised.
2. Boxer.
3. "I will work harder."
4. Mollie and the cat
5. Benjamin the donkey
6. flag-raising, general meeting and singing, recreation
7. green with a hoof and a horn, comparable to the red Soviet flag with a hammer and sickle
8. Snowball and Napoleon
9. Snowball
10. Some animals attained marginal literacy, but saw little use for it. It was to the pigs' advantage to keep the animals from learning too much.
11. Snowball/ "Four legs good, two legs bad."/ the sheep
12. Napoleon
13. The milk and apples were being consumed by the pigs. Squealer explained they needed this "brain food."
14. Jones would come back.
15. student opinion
16. a. The use of "comrade" implies equality and friendship.
    b. The words to the song provided a sense of unity and purpose.
    c. Snowball was able to convince the birds their wings counted as legs.
    d. Squealer convinces the animals that apples and milk are brain food needed by the pigs. (Student answers to this question may vary.)
17. Better off (sample answers):
    a. no more bits, chains, whips, etc.

b. feelings of pride and optimism for the future
c. more to eat due to better productivity

18. Worse off (sample answers):
    a. They are unwittingly slaves to the pigs.
    b. They do not share the benefits of the farm equally.

Chapter 4

1. Pigeons were sent with word to animals on neighboring farms.
2. Foxwood Farm, owned by easy-going Pilkington, was run-down and neglected. Pinchfield, owned by the shrewd Mr. Frederick, was smaller but better kept.
3. The animals on other farms sang "Beasts of England."
4. the pigeons
5. Snowball, who was in charge of defensive operations.
6. Pigeons and geese pecked, sheep butted, and then there was a false retreat. Once the intruders were lured into the barnyard they were charged by the horses, cows and remaining pigs. Snowball was wounded and a sheep killed, while Boxer knocked a stable-boy unconscious. The men retreated.
7. "The only good human is a dead one" was said by Snowball.
8. Mollie was discovered missing but was found hiding in her stall.
9. Snowball and Boxer received the medal of "Animal Hero, First Class" while the dead sheep was awarded "Animal Hero, Second Class."
10. Rebellion: Midsummer Day; Battle of the Cowshed: October 12

Chapter 5

1. Mollie allowed one of Pilkington's men to stroke her nose. She was later seen in town wearing a ribbon and eating sugar.
2. Snowball and Napoleon agreed on almost nothing. Snowball won over the majority with his speeches, while Napoleon canvassed for support in between meetings.
3. Drown out the crucial parts of Snowball's speeches.
4. Snowball developed the idea for the windmill, so Napoleon was against it. It would supply electricity and heat and do much of the work now being done by the animals, but it would be a great deal of work to build it.
5. He urinated on them.
6. The animals seemed to agree with whoever was speaking.
7. Napoleon had his nine fierce dogs chase Snowball off the farm.
8. Jessie and Bluebell's puppies, nearly grown and trained to be vicious
9. They ended.
10. Squealer was the "propaganda" representative, sent to keep the animals appeased.
11. They believed him, mostly out of fear of Jones coming back.
12. "Napoleon is always right."
13. Old Major's skull
14. This is symbolic of the pigs' rise in power.
15. The windmill was to be built after all.
16. to get rid of Snowball, who is dangerous and a bad influence
17. three growling dogs

Chapter 6

1. Rations would be reduced by half.
2. They felt they were working for their own good and that of other animals who would come after them.
3. how to break the stones/They ended up dropping them from the top of the quarry.
4. Boxer's strength was essential in dragging the stones up the hill.
5. paraffin oil, nails, string, dog biscuits, iron for horseshoes
6. trade with neighboring farms
7. hay, wheat, eggs
8. A broker, Mr. Whymper, would be used as a go-between.
9. sly, with side whiskers, and smart enough to realize he could make good commissions
10. Squealer
11. They had developed a certain respect for the animals' efficiency.
12. that he was about to enter into a direct agreement with either Pilkington or Frederick
13. into the house; They are becoming more like the humans they supposedly despise.
14. He said the commandment was only against beds with sheets.
15. The work is being done by others. Pigs are getting more privileges all the time.
16. It was found in ruins.
17. student opinion/Snowball

Chapter 7

1. to make it harder to destroy
2. Boxer and Clover
3. Napoleon
4. Animals were instructed to casually remark within his hearing that rations had been increased; empty bins were almost filled with sand, then grain.
5. rarely appears in public; guarded at all times by dogs
6. that they died of coccidiosis (a disease)
7. on one of the neighboring farms
8. As he vacillated about who to sell the timber to, Snowball was always said to be hiding on the other farm.
9. most of the animals, but Boxer in particular
10. Napoleon says so.
11. Four pigs confessed they had been secretly in touch with Snowball. Three hens said Snowball had incited them to disobey. A sheep confessed to fouling the drinking pool, while other sheep confessed to murder. All were slaughtered.
12. that everyone should work harder
13. After the confessions, she began singing "Beasts of England." She would continue to do whatever she was told to prevent the return of human beings.
14. With the Rebellion completed, it is no longer needed. Another song, written by Minimus, replaced it.
15. the sheep chanting

Chapter 8

1. It shows how the animals were supposed to idolize Napoleon, and it is full of propaganda about how "wonderful" he is and life on the farm is.
2. The words "without cause" have been added.
3. The rumors kept alive the anger which fueled the animals' belief in the farm.
4. "Death to Frederick"
5. spearheading a plot among the hens to murder Napoleon; mixing weed seeds with the seed corn
6. It was originally Snowball's idea, and the source of their greatest conflict.
7. He is unspeakably cruel to his animals; his bank notes for the lumber were no good.
8. Fifteen men marched in with guns and the animals retreated; the men blew up the windmill; the animals were so angry they drove the men out, but many animals were killed or wounded.
9. They are merely celebrating keeping what they had to begin with.
10. They get drunk, and believe Napoleon is dying when he develops a hangover.
11. Barley will be sown there, presumably to make whiskey.
12. to add "to excess" to the fifth commandment

Chapter 9

1. Boxer has a split hoof. Clover treats him with poultices and urges him to work less.
2. less than a year
3. a "readjustment" of rations
4. yes
5. A school is built for the young pigs; the pigs and dogs eat better food than the others; other animals must step aside to let pigs pass; pigs wear green ribbons on Sunday; pigs now drink beer regularly.
6. Like human "fat cats," their leisurely lifestyle is making them fat. Ironically, humans would find them more valuable this way (as meat).
7. a celebration of the struggles and triumphs of Animal Farm
8. He was the only candidate.
9. that the wounds were inflicted by Napoleon
10. "Sugarcandy Mountain" represents heaven. It has once again become the only real hope for the animals.
11. the windmill and the schoolhouse
12. He is actually sending him to the knacker, but wants the other animals to believe he is kind.
13. Squealer claims the knacker's truck was bought by the veterinarian, but he hadn't yet had time to repaint it. The animals believe him.
14. They use Boxer as an example of a fine comrade and worker.
15. from the knacker

Chapter 10

1. Clover, Benjamin, Moses, and some of the pigs
2. no/student opinion
3. None of the rewards have materialized.

4. paperwork
5. Benjamin remembers every detail of his life and knows that things never had been much better or much worse.
6. "Four legs good, two legs better!"/because the pigs are now walking on their hind legs
7. "All animals are equal, but some animals are more equal than others."
8. Napoleon wears Jones' clothes and drinks beer, feeds the animal-workers meager rations, walks on two legs, plays cards.
9. The pigs and the neighboring farmers toasted a future in which all would cooperate. Animal Farm was admired because its animals did more work and received less food than anywhere else in the county.
10. When the animals look at the pigs and humans, they can't tell them apart.